New York to Okinawa Slooooowly

New York to Okinawa Slooooowly

JOHN BARNES

Order this book online at www.trafford.com
or email orders@trafford.com

Most Trafford titles are also available at major online book retailers.

Printed in the United States of America.

ISBN: 978-1-4269-5656-0 (sc)
ISBN: 978-1-4269-5657-7 (hc)
ISBN: 978-1-4269-5658-4 (e)

Library Of Congress Control Number: 2011902021

Trafford rev. 03/29/2011

 www.trafford.com

North America & International
toll-free: 1 888 232 4444 (USA & Canada)
phone: 250 383 6864 ♦ fax: 812 355 4082

TURN OF EVENTS

Graduation

Enlistment U.S.C.G

Boot Camp Bound

Long Beach Island, N.J. next stop

Disaster, Good Friend Lost

Transfer to Buoy Tender Lilac

Radio School, Atlantic City, NJ

Another Transfer to Patrol Frigate 18

Off to Miami, FL   AOG 34

Rahway N.J. next

Our Ship Delivered. Shakedown Cruise. Oops

Bermuda Triangle

Arrival in Aruba

Panama Hot Hot

San Pedro, California

The Mighty Pacific

Hawaii-Pearl Harbor for us

On the move again - Back to Sea

Mog Mog, in the Marshall Islands

Ulithe, in the Caroline Islands

OKINAWA-Typhoon after typhoon Japs swarming our way
Battleship Penna. takes Kamakazi hit (next to us

Atom Bomb causes Jap SURRENDER

Going on Troop ship to California, Train to Philadelphia & HOME

Our 1941 Graduation Class was full of enthusiasm, as well as some misgivings, and rightly so. There were not many decent jobs in these depression days for untrained high school graduates. Some were planning on College, but a lot of us were not able to afford Collage. Our first option was to seek work in our local steel mill, which was known to be miserable work, other than that, who knows. In any event, overall it had been a great year. Our football team was the undefeated State of Delaware champions, which was a first for our smallish school. In addition to that, there had not been any major problems among our community and us with the exuberance of youth we moved on in various directions.

The war in Europe did not figure in our plans. Weren't they always fighting over there? I was born shortly after World War 1 ended. Between either advancing our education and/or working, in addition to our active dating routine we did not have time to become concerned. So when Don, our class president, unquestionably the most popular kid in the school told us he and Ken had gone to Canada and signed up for flight school, it came as a shock, they both wanted to be Fighter Pilots.

They jumped the gun on the rest of us by at least six months. PEARL HARBOR, what the hell did those crazy Japs think they were doing attacking one of our protectorates? Then the bad news kept coming in, they had attacked from the air and sunk several of our Battleships, killed a lot of our sailors and solders too because they shot our airfield up. Now they caught our attention, three of my classmates enlisted the next day.

My choice was the Marines, but my Mother would not sign for me, I was eighteen and could not sign myself. An older cousin took his families 46 ft. boat, and he with his boat was made Chief Petty Officer. He was to patrol the Delaware River on submarine patrol. Captain Coffin, commander of the fourth navel district set the deal up for them. My aunt and uncle were his drinking buddies, connections do help. Anyway, I had always looked up to my cousin Frank, so I decided if the Coast Guard suited him, I too would join. Therefore, off to Philly I went to sign up.

A bunch of us were told to remove out clothes in the adjoining room and wait. Rumors about sitting naked on a marble bench turned out to be true, rather than get a frozen behind we all stood up and waited. After that indignity, the Doctor who was to examine us arrived. He ordered us to form three lines about ten feet apart, then bend down and grab our ankles, at which time be walked slowly behind each row and had a good look. After that, the rest of the exam was a snap, except for one thing, I was given a prescription to go to this certain Doctor in Wilmington and be circumcised. I had always thought that only Jewish people had that done. Following the "operation", I was to report to Philadelphia in ten days.

While backing out of the Doctor's narrow driveway, there was an old fashion hairpin fence on my left side, my pecker hurt so damn much I could not turn around to back up, I just used the rear view mirror. I must have nipped the fence and one whole section fell over. The crabby Doctor came running out and was mad as the devil. I tried, but there was no way for me to put up the fence by myself, not in my condition, my cousin gave me a hand with it and that closed that episode.

Get this! My girlfriends Mother felt sorry for me, and said I was safe so I could sleep with her daughter so she could console me, which she did and the pain became bearable. For the next couple of days I was compelled to walk straight legged, the fellows thought it was funny, but there was no humor as far as I was concerned. Oh! Well! All in the service of our great country. The pain did lessen, and in ten days, it was back to Philadelphia.

The same group was resembled and after a short wait, we were loaded on a bus beaded south. As in any group, there were various opinions as to where we might be going, our temporary new home was to be U. S. Coast Guard training center in Curtis Bay, Maryland. As the bus pulled in the gate there was a bunch of clowns who welcomed us with "you'll be sorry." Okay, our turn will come later, for the moment we were nothing but pathetic boots, the lowest of the low.

Upon leaving the bus, we were hustled to what I guess you would call a supply shack. We were issued our uniforms, which included work dungarees and chambray shirts, undress white uniforms, dress blue uniforms including navy active shirts, underwear, shoes, and socks. Then in a Quonset hut, which included bath, we were assigned to our bunks in alphabetical order. A First Class Boson Mate told us we were Company B, and he was in command.

My bunkmates name was Arthur Carlin, it didn't take long for us to be acquainted, but before we were able to secure our clothing we were hustled off for our shots. A nurse on one side and a Doctor on the other, they lined us up and started punching away. Seven shots, four on one side and three on the other. A couple of the men ahead of me passed out, but I managed not to embarrass myself, thank goodness, came close though. The nurse left a needle that looked better suited for a horse banging in my punctured arm while she reached for a bandage. It did not take her long to return, but that was one mean looking device.

After the shots, they had us to out to the parade field, where we were all assembled and an older Lieutenant Junior Grade took charge of us. It seemed cruel at first until the kindly old man (yeah he was, as we were soon to find, he was a rarity) anyway he explained that it hurts now, but if we did not do the calisthenics it would pain much longer. When the old boy left us, one of our men said I think we should name him "port side Benson" because his head leaned sharply to the left.

We were to become very familiar with the parade ground, they marched us for hours at a time. The drillmaster seemed hard on us at first, but we were raw "boots" and they wanted to toughen us up a bit, he was obnoxious as hell, but I suppose his job required it. To tell the truth, much to my surprise, as we started to get better I enjoyed it. Stepping out smartly and reacting to the commands was not bad at all, especially on Saturday when we were allowed to march to the dress parade. It gave you a thrill as an insignificant person receives when he feels he is never the less a part of the tremendously power force. We're gonna kick those Japs ass!! If that sounds a bit corny coming from a new recruit, who has not done a thing yet, that is how I feel when marching with hundreds of others with a darned good band. There is a name for jerks like me, Go git em!

In addition to the marching we studied basic seamanship, the rules of the road, knot tying, seaaphora (wigwagging) messages visually, from ship to ship or whatever, etc.. Salute the colors before boarding a ship, etc... Shine your shoes, do not wear your hat on the back of your head, square it over your eyebrows when on liberty, or anywhere, I suppose. What do I know, I am only a lowly apprentice seaman.

One night a couple of the guys would not shut up after lights out at ten. The Company Commander turned the lights on at 3AM and told us to roll our mattress up and go outside, he told us to hold the mattress over our head, and he made us run around the drill field three times. The talkers got the message, because the rest of us pushed the point.

The obstacle course was a part of out training. Most of us young eager ones managed to handle it fairly well, but there was one 'old' (40 years old), seemed very old to us youngins. He felt strongly about joining up and doing his part, and we admired him for it. The hell of it was the poor guy would flunk out if he could not handle the obstacle course. So myself, as well as others would boost him up over the wall, or pull him through the pipe, he managed to finish.

Of course, we had no inkling as to where we might be going. A lot of us were hoping for a ship, we depression kids had seen precious little travel. The furthest north I had been was Philly, and the family did manage a trip to Washington, D. C. That trip was funny, my Father had never driven in a busy city before, he pulled up behind this car and waited and waited until my Mother spoke up and said, "John what the hell are you waiting for?" My Father said, "That dumbbell ahead of me" Mother said, "You're the dumbbell," that car is parked.

When we awoke the next morning, we were told to pack our sea bags after breakfast. After breakfast, they told us to board the waiting bus. What next? The Jersey shore was looming up in the distance, the driver told us Long Beach Island.

We were brought in to replace the army fellows who would be moving out that day. It was supposed to have been Coast Guard work, but we lacked the personnel until now. "Boat's" the 1st Class Boatswain who had driven us explained there were seven stations on the Island and each patrolled two miles of beach. Most of the stations had been nearly filled; we were just to fill in as needed starting at the southern end of the Island and working north. My former bunkmate Arthur and I thought we would wait before volunteering to get off. The driver informed us there were two more stops, each requiring one. At best, my good friend would be two miles away, what a screw up!

At least there was some consolation, because the rest of the places that men were dropped off looked so remote. Nothing but some beachfront homes in sight, whereas there was a little town near my stop, the St. Rita's Hotel, a small one but a block off the beach.

The Chief Boatswain who was in charge had the 1st class who had been our driver set me up on the second floor in a room for two, not bad lodging for a seaman. Dinner was served at five in the mess hall (dinning room to you), unless you were on the four to eight watch, than you were fed earlier. My first watch would be eight to twelve (eight hundred to twelve hundred), wear leggings. The beaches are covered with oil from all the tankers being sunk just offshore. Therefore, there was something going on here!

The beach pounders, as they called themselves filled me in. We walk to the oily beach, they tell me one carries a 03 Springfield rifle, one carries a World War relic, the other one carries a 38 revolver strapped on. Our basic purpose is to watch for Germans, dropping off spies in rubber boats. A U-boat would lay off shore at night and drop them off. Some civilians would not observe blackouts properly and there would be a beam showing making a target for the Subs out there. We were authorized to make them cover up.

I mentioned before there were seven stations, each covering two miles of beach. When the truck drops you off, first thing is to clock in, then you and your partner walk one mile along the beach punch the clock, walk the second mile and punch again. Repeat this in reverse and your four hours of beach pounding is completed, the same is repeated in twelve hours. I had been told when the tide is out you have hard sand to walk, but when the tide is in you have to trudge along in the sand. There is a phone line behind the dune that is a private line to all the stations. In the event of seeing a rubber boat land in the dark, one man is to go behind the dunes and advise that a German has come ashore. The other man is to not to shoot and stay out of sight, they must be alive for possible interrogation. There are enough of us so that you work two shifts a day; seven days a week, then you get a two-day weekend liberty off every other week. That covers our duties.

The next day my 8 to 12 walk was interesting, looking at the mostly beautiful oceanfront homes. The down side, because of being new they stuck me with a contrary so and so who did not say a word the whole time. Lucky me, silence makes the time drag, I hope they revolve partners. I am a talker and conversation is sorely missed, maybe he will soften in time. Hope I am not stuck with him too long.

The truck picked us up at four and took us back to the barracks, where we turned our weapons in. Twice a day fresh weapons are exchanged for ones that have been on the beach for twelve hours, the blowing sand makes this necessary. We went to the garage to remove the oily leggings, and change to clean shoes. When we returned the place was buzzing and everybody seemed somewhat upset. They had just received a phone call from the station below us.

Art and his partner were waiting to turn their weapons in, and were sitting across from each other at a table, and Art's partner decided to play cowboy. He picked the loaded weapon up, aimed it at Art and shot him in the head. The crazy son of a bitch killed him! The first day on patrol and a special young guy is no more, I feel so sorry for his parents. That's one day I will never forget, what a senseless damn shame.

Except once on our 8 to 12 walk, my silent companion started to walk away, he was going past the last key post, and the only thing between us and the end of the island was one last house in this wild looking remote place, beyond that you could see Atlantic City on the other side of the inlet. I follow him to the side door of this remote house and knocked. A little old lady let us in, her warmth matched the warmth of her kitchen. Then she busied herself serving piping hot tea and cookies. What a welcome treat that was, coming in from the cold. Everybody held her in very high esteem, so at Christmas we all chipped in and literally filled the bed of a pickup truck with canned goods, enough for a year. She never missed her opportunity to serve "her boys." What a dear lady.

I'm alone now, my roommate is on the beach. The horror of the way that nineteen year old Art departed, tears me up. The damned fool that shot him must be suffering plenty.

For a while the silent walks continued without relief. Then one dark moonless night, making the beach more spooky that ever, there was aloud noise and lights overhead, it gave us quite a start. It turns out that the boys from the Naval Air Station nearby, who were out patrolling in a blimp, had cut their engine and lights and guided over our heads. They too were bored, I suppose. Cute trick, very funny I thought. After that fear wore off another thing happened, a new walking partner. Happy Day. Sam and I hit it off fine and that made the walk seem easier.

One night, not on our patrol, two other guys said they were approaching the area where the old pier had stood, and only the pilings remained. They said something didn't look right even though it was dark, when they looked closer they realized the Chief was checking up on them, and was sort of hiding, they fired a single shot over the ocean. The Chief came running out from among the pilings waving his hat and yelling, it's me. They were not punished because he was apparently aware he had made a foolish mistake.

Three months has gone by and here I am only 70 miles from home. What to do ask for a transfer? I told the Chief I was looking to serve aboard a ship, darned if he didn't turn me loose promptly. He gave me my orders to report to Coast Guard "Lilac" in Edgemore, Delaware. Lilac was a cutter, and I could not get there fast enough. The homeport was close to my home, which I knew, but they would be traveling away, I hoped. As I walked down the gangway to go aboard, I stopped midway to salute the colors, and the Captain was watching me from the bridge. Did I imagine he winked at me, or did it actually happen? No sooner had I gotten aboard when three of the crew accosted me. They told me the Captain was a great guy and would do anything that he could for you, so don't screw up, their meaning was quite clear. Observing the Captain in the future, I was able to see that he had a nervous eye twitch. After I was assigned to a bunk, the 1st Class Boatswain told me I would be the starboard tang man.

The Lilac was a hard working little ship, and after two days, she took off down the Delaware River toward the Ocean. The Helmsman really had the feel of the ship's wheel, after backing into mid river; he swung that big wheel five full turns. The ship responded just as we were going straight down the river. Hey! This is fun, some people cannot operate a car that well. When we came to the car ferry's that is when you want to see some fun. One ferry is loading on the New Castle side in Delaware, while another is loading cars on the New Jersey side. Meanwhile there are two other loaded ones on their way. These ferries move at a good clip, and our ship slipped adroitly in between them and made it look easy.

About forty miles down river, we stopped at a little country town called Smyrna. We took on a crew of five and their provisions for a month. Another forty miles opened to the Delaware Bay. At this junction, there was a lightship, which is permanently anchored at this point. A light buoy is stationed where it can be seen for many miles, just like a lighthouse on land. This Coast Guard vessel was named the Overfalls. The crew told us she was round bottom and when a storm hit the bay, she did a lot of rolling and pitching. The fresh crew was put aboard and the ones finishing their thirty-day stay came aboard our ship. They were looking forward to their thirty days off now. As the fresh food supply was put aboard, the crew filled their tank and away we went down to the ocean, it was now close.

Just before going into the Atlantic we tied up at a coastal town called Lewes, Delaware. This is a quaint little town settled by the Dutch in the early seventeenth century. We dropped the lighthouse crew off here and took a crew of hardhat divers aboard who had come down from the Philadelphia Navy Yard.

We made our way a few miles at sea and ran into a problem. We were to check out the "descaving" run, an electrical cable on the ocean floor that checked ships that ran over to be sure they were not "positive" to attract enemy mines as the ship passed over them. The intruder was a newly commissioned ship built in the Philly Yard. She was a "Heavy Cruiser," meaning heavier guns, up to eight inches were aboard, the USS Boise was a beautiful sight running back and forth over the cable. This beauty obviously had priority over us, so we had to get out of the way and wait. Wait, we did as we rolled around standing by for three days. The Divers got as sick as could be. Eventually the Boise went to join the fleet and the divers were able to complete their job of checking the system out. We put them ashore in Lewes and they were happy campers to get off our ship.

After dropping off the divers we went out to sea again. The sea buoys needed attention, and that was our job. The first buoy was positioned off Atlantic City, N.J. The buoy was bobbing quite a bit, and a gutsy fellow named Chet from Boston, timed the motion of the buoy and jumped aboard, he attached a hook to the upper frame and the boom took up the slack. Now my responsibility was to hold my rope, called a tang and allow slack off the big cleat it was looped around. This one and a half ton buoy was raised, and as the boom started to swing I slacked my line off to keep the load from swinging in out of control. The buoy was then laid on the deck and the five fathoms (fathom six foot) of chain was brought aboard laying it out carefully, and finally the three ton block that holds the buoy on station. Being a sea buoy with a light, a new can was used to replace the nearly empty one. The buoy is then scrubbed and painted if required. The buoy is picked up, and the tang man on the other side lets his slack out of control to swing overboard. Finally, the exact position is determined by the bridge and the buoy is set back on station. This procedure was repeated off Atlantic City and Wildwood, New Jersey, and Rehoboth, Delaware. A dangerous job well done.

The light buoy was good for another month, with the descaving run serviced and three buoys serviced and repositioned. The Lilac was also classed as an icebreaker, and the river had iced up while we were at sea. The old gal broke up the ice alright, but the noise of the ice breaking on the steel hull of the ship was not conductive to sleep so we had a noisy ride that night.

The Captain was standing on the wharf the next day in port. I told him it had been several months now and I had not had leave yet. The old gentleman said, "How much time do you have coming?" I replied, ten days sir. He said, "Son, tell the Yeomen how much time you have coming, and I will sign the papers, the man was a prince.

The leave was up and I reported aboard ship, fortunately the ship had been working and was back in port. Several days passed and the Yeoman stuck his head in the door of the galley as we were having breakfast, and said we have been notified that there was an opening for one man to go to radio school. Immediately, I said I would go, so just like that, the Yeoman drew up the travel papers and I was on my way. The radio school turned out to be in Atlantic City, New Jersey. Now I am feeling guilty again, here I am only sixty miles away from home, and many of the fellows I grew up with were overseas. I also felt bad about leaving the Lilac, and the good experience from the great Captain on down. They were good congenial hard working crew, and will be missed.

Atlantic City, one block to the boardwalk and the steel pier right here. The Hotel Morton was great, four to a room, and the food was good. I rented a space for eight dollars a month behind the hotel, when I went to pay; she doubled the price to sixteen dollars. I went to the commander of the hotel (he also happened to be the mayor of Atlantic City), and he straightened her out.

My roommates were Van from Kalamazoo, Michigan, the song Kalamazoo had just come out recently and Van was a big good-looking guy. Then next was Al, he was old by our standards of nineteen and twenty, Al was twenty seven, he had a pilots license but was hoping for a ship. Last but not least was Bob Carp, a Jewish boy from Brooklyn. Bob had a love of comedy, and to boot we all thought he had a lot of talent, he greatly admired Groucho Marks, and his imitation was hilarious, Bob never became boring.

We had Friday nights off and every other weekend, on the weekends we had to stay but could have a big crap game in our room. It was best suited because we were on the top floor at the end of the hall, as far as you could get from the office. We had one fellow from next door who usually won, his father owned a sweat shop in New York, and he always had plenty of money. When he was down on his luck, he lost heavily, but always had enough to hold out until he got a hot streak, then he would clean up. Everybody wanted to beat him and that's just what he wanted, he wouldn't touch the dice until everybody had their bets in, SUCKERS!!

One Friday night we were going hot and heavy at midnight when the Chief PO who was the Officer Of The Day burst in and grabbed this big pot up and yelled "BEANS" what the hell can you do? Sure we could take it from him but then we would all be on report and we would be much worse off. He only pulled that once in the six months our class was there, but we figured he made a couple hundred or better.

All four of us roommates went out on the town on the boardwalk, the first Friday night we had liberty. We decided to forget the crap game and go to the burlesque, a short walk on the boardwalk, it was a top rated show and very funny, really sharp gals, too, everybody had a good time.

On another Friday break, Bob took a couple of bucks from each of us and AJ suggested we buy a bottle of Rock and Rye. We went to the pier, and came across four girls and invited them to dance. How lucky can you get? That wasn't enough to please Al, he took the bottle into the head and we all took a snort or two, the liquor was strong, but the concoction was very sweet. That accounts for the rock, and a very pleasant evening was on. The band was good and the girls were real good company, not a dog in the bunch.

Jitterbugging tends to warm you up, but now the booze was taking hold, and I began to feel a little dizzy. That was the first time I had ever tasted liquor, and when I looked at the other fellows they appeared sober. I hadn't drunk much, but I felt drunk, this time when I went to the head I puked. That spoiled it for everybody, when I rejoined the party the girls saw that I was drunk and sick, that did it, they dropped us. Can't say I blame them, I was a party pooper. The others were annoyed as the devil with me, so we went back to the Hotel. It looks as though you have to build up a resistance to the stuff, which I obviously would have to acquire, but for a while at least I think I'll forgo the pleasure.

There was also work to be done; the Coast Guard Radio school course lasted six months, while the Navy was only a three months course. I was told that because the coast guard did the international ice patrols way up into the Artic near the North Pole they needed more range in their radio equipment, anyway the story sounded logical. Exactly 140 students started radio school and 70 finished. Now I was a 3rd class radio operator, and had a crow sewed on my uniform with one little stripe.

I returned back to the Lilac, and Paul Kavalow from my class and I took the place of the old 1st class who had been aboard for a long time. He was transferred two days after our arrival. The next day I found myself trying to send a departure message to the base in

Essington, PA, the old radio was an antique, never before had I seen one like it, Some Fun!

This may sound contrived, but here is how it came about. The yeomen came into the mess hall and said, he had a request for a radio man for a PF. That sounded okay, so once more I jumped at the chance to go with a ship going someplace. This time I was to report to Manhattan Beach Naval Base in Brooklyn. I took the train from Wilmington to New Penn Station, went down stairs and waited on the platform for the train. Now I had been told as a boy, that I should step aside and allow ladies to precede me, so when the train doors opened I held back and allowed two ladies to go ahead. They did, and about fifty more shoved their way in, leaving me standing alone as the train pulled out. As if that wasn't enough, when we arrived at the Coney Island stop, some of the characters couldn't wait for the doors to open, they went out the windows. These lessons were all too clear; take care of number one and the hell with the rest. The next stop was Manhattan Beach, I reported to the office, and had sleeping quarters assigned with other men who were to crew the PF 18. I learned that the PF's were a British design ,they were somewhat smaller than a destroyer with a top speed of only 16 knots, but were ideal for helping to protect convoys of only 10 knots.

This was a large base, consisting of sleeping quarters for several hundred, a beautiful parade ground, and my lucky day, a first class gym. Jack Dempsey was in charge, but you only saw him on parade day, which was Saturday morning. Lew Ambers who had been a great fighter at one time holding three different titles worked in the gym with the men. He had us put the gloves on, and then you were to spar with your buddy. My new friend and I had no desire to punch each other in the face, so we just body punched each other, Lew tapped my buddies shoulder and squared off with me, he gave me 3 or 4 lighting shots to my midsection that felt like a steam roller had struck me. No windup, he just shot them from about six inches from his side, another lesson learned. Don't try to fool a world class fighter.

If that wasn't enough for one day, let me tell you what happened next. Bibber McCoy, a leading professional wrestler at the time also worked in the gym. He had a couple of men punch him in the stomach to show the advantage of being in shape. It hurt their fists, not him; he pointed at me, and said now I will show you a wrestling hold. Face me and relax, he said, just duck your head as I come forward and boom, I forgot to duck my head. Actually he did it without warning so I would be relaxed. I think it scared bibber more than me. Are you alright son, he said very worriedly? Stars were popping and spinning around my head, but I assured the old boy I was okay. You know what? In spite of my couple of painful experiences that gym and those two tip top coaches were really a great experience for a young man.

One day instead of our steady diet of marching, we ran around to cadence being called by the drill instructors, and then around some more. One fellow kept telling the DI he had a bad heart, but apparently he thought the guy was just lazy, and continued. That night he died of heart failure, his Jewish funeral was held promptly and our entire company attended. The boys Mother became so distraught that at one point she made a move to jump in the hole with her son. Somehow he must have hidden any heart problems he had from the examining Doctor.

Early Saturday morning was a busy time at the base in preparation for the big show in mid morning. People were collecting outside the fence, waiting for the parade to start. Start it did, and the band sounded great, in spite of myself I found it exhilarating. After the marching we stood at stiff attention. It was a very hot day and we were overheated from the marching. Stretcher bearers stood by, and sure enough one of the marchers here and there had to be carried off.

The old Rear Admiral in charge of the base must had some ham in him, I guess, because he held the proceedings up for dramatic appeal. In any event, when the Admiral finally arrived with his staff displayed out in back of him. It was kind of anti climatic, because the Admiral was a little runt who took mincing steps, the others seemed to do all right. Jack Dempsey had a terrible time trying to keep in step, he had to shuffle his feet occasionally. It gave kind of a bizarre comical air to the activities, but was enjoyable none the less.

While, or I should say before the above came off. The crew of the Wakefield, a Coast Guard troop ship crashed the gate. They simply defied the guards at the gate and refused to do the marching bit. Two Hundred and Forty marching tightly together made quite a spectacle of their own. These fellows had just been plucked out of the ocean a few days ago, they were damned they were going to spend part of their first liberty marching. They pulled it off beautifully, and apparently got away with it.

After a couple of weeks I was given orders to report to #1 Wall Street, Manhattan. (How's that for a distinguished address)? On the top floor the Navy had a radio station that worked our submarines off shore, such as sending orders to proceed to sea, or possible to return to base, etc., they had a full compliment and certainly didn't need me. Apparently some kind soul thought the experience might do me more good than marching.

Christmas was coming and I'm only about seventy five miles from home. One of the Waves who worked in the area seemed very pleasant, so when I asked her to cover for me, (just tell them I had gone to the head if anyone should ask), bless her heart, she agreed. Then over the hill I went, gave myself ten days at home. When I returned I caught her eye, she gave me the okay sign. How's that for a great little buddy!!

When they brought me back to Manhattan Beach, I hoped the PF18 was ready to board. Still no word, I was stalled. Wouldn't that ship ever be completed? Just about then (I know this will sound crazy, but it is exactly the way it happened for the third time). A yeoman came in our barracks and asked me if I wanted a transfer to an AOG. They gave me immediate orders to become attached to the USS Oconee, AOG34. (Many years later I learned through Jean's International shipping library of sorts, the yard that was to build it never did).

Wow, this time I am not going eight or ninety miles from home, it is Miami, Florida for me. They gave me train ticket and instructions that when I arrived in Miami to proceed to the Hotel Everglades. The trip down south on the train was pleasant, and the scenery wonderful. When we arrived in Miami, a cab took me to the Hotel. What a beautiful setting, the hotel enjoys; it fronts on a waterfront lot on Biscayne Bay. A couple of my new shipmates introduced themselves, one of them a giant of a man named Bill Brodie, and he was a native Miamian.

This was a Navy Hotel. I do not mean to complain, but in the coast guard it's a small outfit compared to the Navy and we have a name, and they use it when addressing us. Every few minutes the loud speaker says, "Now hear this" and so on and so on, other than that, everything was good. A couple of days after arrival I had a few hours off, so it was straight to the beach. South Beach surroundings itself was interesting, but the beach and ocean was the best. Up to my neck in water, I looked down and saw my feet as clear as day! On the Jersey and Delaware, the sand seemed courser, but what really made the difference was the beautiful clear water. Now I started a lifetime love of Florida.

There were quite a few Russians at the Navy base, also several PC 110 wooden boats, that for the entire world looked like yachts. We were told that they were being given to the Russian Navy as part of land lease, and they were too small for ocean crossing. They were loaded a couple at a time and be transported on ships overseas and used for limited patrolling.

We did not stay long at the Hotel; I believe it was only about three weeks. The crew for the Oconee was assembled, but before pushing on again, there is one other thing worth mentioning. A hurricane struck Miami. I was hanging around the boat docks when it struck, it was not a major one, but fun to experience anyway.

The complete AOG34 crew was loaded on a train for the north, we knew not where, until we arrived at Rahway, New Jersey. They settled us in Quonset huts in what had been old CCC barracks during the 30's, it was not too bad. There was a pot bellied stove at either end for heat, such as it was, The youngest member of our crew was a kid, I am going to call Robbie 1, because there will be another Robbie later, who we will call Robbie 2.

We had a fellow in the crew who was very much of a hillbilly, both in manner and appearance. He had an old wind up victrola that was portable with him. He played it loud and frequently and he would not shut the damned thing off, his music was all about losing their women. Robbie 1 brought back his portable radio from a weekend liberty, his home was close in New Jersey. Every time the hillbilly would crank up his victrola, Robbie would turn on his portable and drown him out; Glenn Miller, the Dorsey's, etc. This made the hillbilly mad as hell. It so happened that the two of them, along with eight others from our crew went to Sea Girt, New Jersey, for gun practice on the kind of guns we'd have aboard ship. The first night at Sea Grit when he thought everybody was asleep, the hillbilly got up about 3 AM and went to Robbie's bunk and tried to stab him. One of the crew fortunately was awake, and grabbed him and threw him down. Others were awakened and proceeded to beat the bell out of him. That was the end of him, we never saw him again, off to the brig.

Two days after this unfortunate occurrence, we were to pack our sea bags and be prepared to board out just completed ship over in Bayonne, which was not far away. On arrival, the AOG34 looked like a big shoe. Being a tanker, her house was aft, and because the ship was only 250 feet long, she seemed so stubby. Anyway, "my ship that was going somewhere" it was alive and awaiting her crew. The bunks were four high, the bottom was too close to the deck, and I knew from the old Lilac that the blowers blow the dust along the deck and in bed with you at times. The normal bed height bunk was just the right height for the crapshooters to sit on. The most desirable was the third one up.

You only had to stick your feet in one guys face to get in. Number fours were way up under the overhead, and if you jumped up quickly, you might knock your brains out. Having worked that out in my mind, I threw my mattress in the three high, threw my clothes from my sea bag in the locker and felt established in my new home. The next thing I wanted to see, of course, was the radio shack. It was small, we would only have one man at a time in the there, so that did not matter. Our hatch opened unto the wing of the bridge, and the bulkhead had a sliding door to the bridge, and on the other side sat the radar man, at the rear of the bridge. The modern radio transmitter looked powerful enough. You started at the top and tuned six sets down one and into the next lower one until finally you reached full power. There was a giant knife switch mounted on the overhead, which you pushed on to transmit. You had 3 radios to monitor, 500 the international distress would be on speaker at all times, then the standard receiving channel for copying your orders on WAX, the most powerful transmitter in the world, plus another for calling.

So much for that, the next day we left port for a day's shakedown run. We were in the East River and all of a sudden, there was a big jolt. The Captain, we were told later, panicked when we got too close to a gasoline barge and rammed it. Yes, rammed our brand new ship, and sunk the barge. That earned him the name CRASHBOAT COLLINS. Fortunately, the barge did not explode.

Anyway, so off we go into the wild blue Atlantic, heading south for a bit more adventure. It was not long even at our 8-knot speed, that we found ourselves off the Jersey shore. I could not help smiling to myself at the thought of how I was able to break away from the beach. It looked a bit friendlier from this elevation.

In all good time, we arrived at Norfolk Virginia. The ship was to be pulled out in a couple of days, so the port watch was given liberty in Norfolk, the old sailor's town. We were greeted with signs reading "Dogs and sailors not permitted." In a way I cannot blame them, drunken sailors staggering from bar to bar, raucous as all get out, doing their thing. Not to mention fear for the safety of their young, foolish daughters. You know that old saying "Love them and leave them." Then on the other hand, without the sailors, the Navy, and their jobs in the Navy Yards, this just would be another poor hick town, so much for Norfolk. The hull bottom was repaired and repainted at the Navy Yard then was launched and we were sent on our way.

Headed for Bermuda, we were told by the 1st class quartermaster; he kept us informed at every opportunity. He was of Norwegian descent, they usually make for good sailors, and he was no exception. Bermuda sounded real good, this would be our first foreign port. However, we did not just sashay into the port at Bermuda, there were several hundred miles of ocean to traverse first. Years ago, my Mother had told me her Great Uncle John, who was a Sailing Master or Captain, went down in a winter storm off Hatteras with his three-massed schooner. All that was ever found were his wife and daughter floating all tied to the Mast including Uncle John. The first day was a bit rough, but not unbearable, this trip was expected to take about three days. On day two, one of the guys in the black gang in the engine room turned on the wrong valve, and pumped seawater into our diesel fuel. So now, the ship would idle in the water rolling from side to side.

Bad news now, one of the Hatteras famous storms is overtaking us from astern. The sky is black and the wind is coming up, it's the dreaded nor' eastern, which I have experienced from land, but this is a lot different. By late afternoon of this second day the seas were getting fiercer by the hour, the roll is becoming more pronounced. The waves have grown from five to around twenty five feet in the early evening. Of course the engines injectors were fouled when salt water was introduced to our diesel engine. The black gang below must have cleaned them up, because we're under way again. Now the ship has changed course a bit, and with our headway we can now quarter the seas. This makes for a let up from the severe rolling. When I stepped out of the radio shack when my 4 to 8 watch was completed, salt water struck me in the face. The winds were so strong now that it's blowing the tops of the waves off. By the time I got below the ships engine stopped again. Now we're in big trouble, Sven the quartermaster tells us the waves are about 50 feet high. Our ship is lying in the trough between waves. Then the next wave turns our helpless ship over on it side, we're rolling up to 48 degrees to starboard, back down the other side of the wave, into the trough, then picked up by the next wave and rolled to port before crashing down again. Sven says the ships papers say that the maximum roll she can sustain is 46 degrees. Most everybody is sick now because of the severe roll. You can feel the ship quiver and shake now. I couldn't stand the sea sickness below decks, so I went up to the boat deck and lay down on the ammunition box. It's just about the size of a casket, which seemed appropriate. Now at least I'm getting lots of fresh sea air. When we fall back into the trough I can look almost straight up, and the next wave is going to sink us. At this point I'm so damned sick I wish we would just sink.

A couple of hours on the ammo box were enough, so I went below to try and get a little sleep, at least. Bad idea, the ship would fare a little better when the boys below got her moving again, but the pattern now seemed to be 4 or 5 hours under way, sort of, 4 or 5 hours when we just lay and roll, lay and roll. There was no way to sleep in my bunk; it was just too confined and stuffy in there. So, the galley is a little closer to the center of the ship and there will be others there to talk to. Anyway, I am going to need help getting up those stairs to the radio shack when my 4 to 8 PM watch comes up. The jokesters were quiet for a change.

Well this is it, time for my watch. I have Chuck empty the puke bucket. This is the second night watch, the first one was bad enough, but the weather seems to be at its peak now. A couple of my sick buddies, one either side of me, sort of dragged me up and plunked me in the chair. Chuck said it was quiet on the air, I just had the Fox schedule headings to copy. (Fox puts us in touch with headquarters in California). We copy the headings of the messages they broadcast clear across the Pacific. If our coded call sign (changes every day is not in the heading, we don't have to copy the body of the message, so you get a break between messages. When the next one comes I grab the typewriter platen with one hand because of the ships motion and hold on to it, and type with the other hand.

Working these 4 on 8 off watches is usually a snap, but when you are unable to eat or sleep it becomes quite a chore. The word from the bridge is that we should be able to arrive in Bermuda in 24 to 36 hours. If we can just keep the engine running, what has become six hours of running, six hours of lying dead in the water rolling like crazy?

When I'm off watch my favorite spot is directly behind the engine exhaust, which is about the middle of the ship. That's where you get the least motion, and there is some protection from the wind. We keep hoping the storm will let up, but it just isn't happening. Sliding the panel and talking to the radar man gives me some relief. The poor guy says if he has to watch that radar screen pitch and roll he's going to go crazy, he said, it makes him dizzier.

You know, this little ship with 77 souls aboard may be slow, 8 knots is certainly pokey, but I'm glad that she is also a tough little devil to withhold together in this storm. Many many ships have gone down in weather like this, not to mention being off half of the time.

That was the notorious Bermuda Triangle we transversed in six days, as opposed to a normal two or three days.

Well, 24 hours of being sick and miserable and the storm was at least easing up. A little later on the 6th day it was LAND HO! The island of Bermuda was in sight over the horizon, WHAT A WELCOME SIGHT. A couple of more hours and we have it made. One hour later we come within the "lee" of the island and the sea has eased up a lot.

That was a major improvement, I was told to ask that a tug be sent out for us. The engine was fouled and wouldn't start. A huge sea tug, all of about 120 feet came out and gave us a heavy hawser to pull us in. All went will until he reached his cruising speed of about 12 knots with us in tow. Then our hydraulic steering quit, now we had no power or steering. About then the tug made a sharp turn to starboard, our ship continued to go straight ahead, and the prow cut the hawser. The tug crew screamed to us that we were drifting into the mine field used to protect the harbor. There wasn't a solitary thing we could do. When he pulled several knots beyond what our ship was designed to do he made us helpless, No need to dwell on this, the fact is we were very lucky. We drifted clear through the mine field, and the tug picked us up on the other side. Had we had more draft the mines would have been ignited.

Our drinking water had been fouled five or six days without water had dehydrated us, my tongue had swollen. When we informed the tug crew about the lack of water, they passed several 10 gallon jugs of wonderful fresh water to us. We didn't fight over it but we were certainly anxious for our turn to drink. Things were starting to look up, the tug got us secured along the quay side right in the city of Hamilton, Happy Day. Then they moved us into the Navy yard when room was found for us. The Brits told us that because of the overflow of the various military groups the town was over run. Only 20 of the crew would be allowed ashore on liberty at a time, instead of our usual port and starboard one half crews. It kind of rankled us, because on the bulkhead on the other side from us were five Italian Fascist submarines, men ran back and forth to the ships store constantly, buying silk stocking and cigarettes and sending them home. How do you like those apples?

When Bill and I finally did get ashore, it was a great feeling not to be pitched around. Mother earth felt very good! Hamilton Bermuda was a most welcome stop after that wild trip over. The city itself was very interesting, the only automobile on the island belonged to the Governor. Small cycles scooted about, but nothing larger. Hamilton enjoyed fronting on the harbor, which can enrich any town, plus the British feel gave it the foreign flavor all travelers enjoy. The atmosphere was such that even the sailors behaved well. There is of course a lot more to Bermuda, one of the local people was telling about their houses being built over a cistern. Water from the roof was guided down rainspouts and into the cellar. Water could be a major, or should I say lack of, in a severe dry spell. There is so much to enjoy, I'm sure, maybe another time. At least this one trip ashore was worthwhile. Times up, back to the ship.

In a couple of days, we were on our way again, to we know not where. The Panama Canal is almost a straight shot south from Bermuda. Old Sven the quartermaster came through for us again; it is great having a direct connection with the bridge and what is going on. Our next stop is to be Aruba, a Dutch occupied island off the coast of Venezuela, South America, Southward Ho! Hang on, because the best is yet to come. When we radioed in for dockage and the dock master asked what our cargo was, he was told aviation gasoline. With that knowledge in hand, he had no choice but to send us far to anchor about a half mile offshore. He said, "He didn't want to blow up the city". Once we had the hook down they sent a livery boat to bring anyone who wanted to go to town, a bunch of us piled aboard and were taxied in. The little narrow houses were very quaint; all the colors of the rainbow were seen. Oil was the big thing here in Aruba. The whites lived on top of a high hill on the far end of town, I gathered the sailors would not be welcome there, so did not attempt it. The town had two things besides their quaintness, booze and sex, the booze in the bars of course. The whores and the taxi drivers paired up, they ride down the street saying "beachie beachie". One of the crew who took a fling on this dubious pleasure said they were doing a big business. When their cab came to halt at the beach they would fling the door open and run. It turned out there were a lot of stickers on the beach, and the girls didn't want to plant their posterior in those blighted areas. These women were sent from Venezuela for a thirty day period, and then fresh "stock" was used to replace them. This was their big earnings opportunity, and they were thankful to get it. Not having a desire for the commodes offered, I decided it was time to return to the ship. (If I sound a bit prudish, movies that shown bandages being pulled off someone's penis, with lots of flesh sticking to it had erased any remote desire, Syphilis, or even gonorrhea just didn't turn me on). When I arrived at the dock the Chief of Police was there, he wanted to know if I was off the Oconee, when I answered affirmably he told me when I got back to the ship I was to tell the captain, "his whole damn crew was in jail, they had gotten drunk and tried to tear the town up". Since I appeared sober he sent me along with his message. This shouldn't bother the Captain too much, according to the stewards who tidied the Captains cabin up. He had liquor piled up in cases anywhere there was room, under his bunk, in the closet, wherever. Sure enough when I reported back to the ship I thought the hint of a smile crossed his face. That appeared to be the end of it, and the pharmacists mates never had any leaks in their plumbing. So we leave Aruba two days later and head again for the open sea. To close that segment out, the 1st class gunners mate said, "Any time I want to leave this ship I have a strain that looks just like the clap, and I can bring it on any time I want to". Sure enough, at the next port he was dropped off, no, the second port, I believe it was, and he was gone.

Around the top of South America we go, we crept along at our steady 8 knots and arrived at our next port in about three days, I believe it was. Colon, our next port was on the Atlantic side of the Panama Canal. We immediately became aware of the heat as soon as we arrived. Our ship didn't have air conditioning, of course, only blowers that pushed outside air and circulated it, usually it worked alright but this place overpowered it. The ship acted like a giant radiator, it soaked up heat during the day and radiated it all night. The second day our port watch went ashore. There were a lot of locals selling chances on something, but the big business was, you guessed it, prostitution. There were lines encircling the block for entrance to the state owned whore house. It looked as though the dirty little city had been carved out of the surrounding jungle. So, back to the ship and another night to look to in the incessant heat, so much for colon. That night I had a 4 AM watch, so when I was relived at 8, I had a bit of breakfast and went to bed. Sleep was a welcome relief from the heat. When I woke up and went up on deck one of the guys asked where I had been, I told him about the 4 to 8 watch and sleep. Well you managed to sleep clear through the canal, we are now entering the Pacific Ocean, so be it. Next stop San Diego, California.

Goldie was my immediate boss. He was a 1st class radio man, but he didn't sit any watches. His job primarily, as material men was to maintain the radio equipment and set out watches, etc. He had been a musician before the war, said he played tenor sax for Jack Teagarden, a so called musicians musician. Goldie and I made our liberty together in San Diego. Goldie's suggestion was that we see a show and have a really good dinner. It was a pleasure to be in a real city, with lots of activity and things to do, but one thing bothered us. Very young kids, they all seemed to be teenagers, were trying to pick up servicemen. In a lot of cases, I guess both their parents are working in the aircraft industry and these children slip out at night. Goldie has a small daughter at home and it really disturbed him to see this. There is a potential for diseases on both sides, and the potential for a lot of fatherless babies being left behind.

Otherwise it is a beautiful southern California night out and a great place to enjoy it in. Goldie suggested we walk back to the ship, it took us 4or 5 hours, but when you spend most of your time restricted to 200 feet of deck, it's a treat to take a long walk for a change.

Two days later I had another liberty, this time Bill and I went into San Diego. With this bland diet we have on board you kind of get a desire for chocolate. What a treat that was, it was the first chocolate in months. I don't know why it is but when you hang out with Big Bill things just seem to happen. Such as, we were walking down the street and saw six marines cross over to our side. As they approached they fanned out and completely blocked the sidewalk. That left a detour into the gutter for the sailor boys. Bill would have none of it, he took a deep breath, swelling that 58....yes, I said that 58 chest inches expanded, and his huge latts swelled for all the world looking like a cobra ready to strike. There was no striking and honestly I don't think there was any meant to be, they just thought they were having fun. The marines opened up in the middle and we sauntered through. They probably hadn't seen the likes of that before; they even turned around for a rear view of this massive man. You see, at 17 years of age he earned his spending money traveling with a carnival as the man who would take on anybody in the ring and if they lasted one round they got $100 dollars.

We bumped into a couple of the crew, Bob Cunningham very much Boston Irish and proud of it, and the pharmacists mate. When they were told about the delicious chocolate milk shake we'd just had, they had to have one, so we joined them for another. Well Bob being Irish and all, although he was a prince of a guy, he tended to be shall I say a little bullheaded. So when his time came to order, he ordered chocolate frappe. The clerk didn't know what the hell he was talking about and frappe being correct in Boston, he wouldn't give the man the proper answer, and we had to order for him. I think the other boys were accustomed to stronger drinks, but we all enjoyed ribbing bullheaded Bob. This would be our last chance to go ashore for awhile, we all knew so we made the best of it before going back to the ship,

The Mighty Pacific was appropriately named. Some of the fellows started hanging out on the flying bridge, way up on top of the ship, where there was a nice sea breeze. The ship executive officer was up there taking sun sights with the sextant. "Wichita Fails" Tex was also up there in all his unwashed glory. He would put on a new pair of dungarees and never take them off. They finally rot off and only then would he replace them. Unfortunately for all of us was that this filthiness developed the crabs. In the head there were 5 or 6 wash basins, a couple of showers and a trough which was a few inches high at the upper end, and water was pumped through constantly with sea water. There were dividers between the six stalls but no doors, Tex, because of his slough was assigned the one at the lower end, and that one only. A nasty trick conceived by somebody. I know not who was to enter the head unnoticed with a piece of paper in hand, light it, drop in the upper end, and listen for the yelp. The odor of burning hair was very strong, even poor dirty Tex did not deserve that.

Back on the flying bridge, the exec was taking navigational sun sights. Tex wanted to talk to him about something, so he continuously pulled at the sleeve of his jacket. He tried to shake Tex off but he was persistent. The kid was incorrigible but he just would not stop shaking, so the exec drew himself up to his unimposing 5 feet 6 inches and said, "Can't you see I am shooting the sun." Tex replied, "I hope you hit the son of a bitch." Of course, we all roared and the officer was furious. You can only fine us two thirds of there monthly wages for a limited time, and that did not mean much because about all you could buy from the ship's store was cigarettes, shaving supplies and not much else. There was no brig on a small ship such as ours, so he went unpunished. In a way, it would be kind of a shame anyway. Tex obviously was not playing with a full deck.

In this same period as we traveled toward Pearl Harbor we all became pretty much outdoorsmen. At night, we would take our mattress and cover out on the catwalk, and it was great to sleep under the stars. Chuck Sipes, one of the other radiomen I worked with got the bright idea one night to move from where he had told me he would be. When I came to call him to relieve me at 4 AM, can you imagine the confusion and anger stepping on others who did not want to be wakened and stepped on while you are trying to find Sipes? Of course my turn came when he least expected it. While I am on the subject, the third member of our exclusive little radio girl (because we typed) group was Anthony Cardillo from New York. Anthony had gone to the semi finals in the amateur boxing matches before being defeated. When he got home that night after finally losing, his father who was a longshoreman beat the hell out of him because he had lost. Would you call that tough love? We had agreed among ourselves that the one who had the 4 to 8 watch each morning would scrub the radio shack, because we all ate in there, and we wanted to keep it clean. One morning Anthony threw the water over the side and a little blew in the porthole right below our wing of the bridge. The exec came up in his underwear looking more like a boy scout and raised the devil with Anthony. The three of us were territorial about our private little area alone off the wing of the bridge. Therefore, like three musketeers, we stood our ground. We knew his bunk was right inside the big porthole, so right then and there we agreed there would be a few more wild winds blowing the water back. There were no more wild tirades aimed at one of us. The stewards told us he had moved his mattress to the other side of his cabin. He was never one of my favorite people.

When we were in Miami everybody that is everybody including officers, who entered the Miami naval facility was sent to take an intelligence test. My turn came, and when he had checked it all out the person who administered it said 34,500 some, odd, had preceded me and I was number two with and IQ of 162. Now I know a lot of people don't put much store in those tests, but I thought he was way out of line when I turned my papers back in with this information attached by the gentleman who had given the tests, and the little bastard tore the paper up and threw it in the wastebasket in his room.

One day the powers to be, decided to test the anti submarine gear. It consisted of a half dozen "ash cans" mounted on an inclined holder. Therefore, the gunner set a depth charge at say 100 feet, at which time the pressure in the sea would set it off. Set it off! All right. There was a huge explosion, the stern of our ship jumped clear out of the water, propeller spinning. We feared for the ship, it was so severe. We did not sink, but also no more depth charges were dropped. We were too slow to move away from the explosion as you are supposed to do. If we were to engage an enemy sub, we would have had to use deck guns instead. Old crash boat Collins at work again.

In the meantime, life on the tanker Oconee goes on. Bill is working out on the fantail with his weights and Goldie is playing his tenor sax. One of the radar men had been an MC and bongo player in a nightclub, he and Goldie sent some beautiful sounds wafting behind in the breeze. Bill pulled me aside and told me our chief Warrant

Officer had taken it upon himself to make sarcastic remarks when we was working out and he had all he was going to take. He is an old peacetime regular, he's probably been in a few bar room set two's and thinks he's manly, and Bill isn't. Man, how stupid can you get. I hung around enjoying the music, and sure enough here struts up Mr. Tough Guy, with a smirk he implied those weights were easy to lift. Bill isn't much for talking, he loaded the bar up with every weight he had, about 300 pounds I surmised, because I had worked out with Bill a few times. Anyway, Bill says, "pick that up" to the Warrant Officer. So, he bends down, grasps the bar and along with a bit of groaning lifts it 6 to 8 inches off the deck. He stood back looking very proud of himself. Bill reached down with his right arm (right arm only, mind you) and grasped the bar in the middle, he made a fluid motion from the deck to up over his head, arm extended full length. As he stood there holding this unbelievable amount of iron over his head he said, "Leave me alone, you son of a bitch". Exit the fool who mixed it up with the big leagues. When we were in the New York area Bill would workout with Sandow, who was at that time officially the strongest man in the world. Bills father was also a professional weight lifter and a good friend of Sandow, so at any time he was in Manhattan Bill was welcome. Our Warrant Officer became quite a joke aboard ship. The tough was anything but brave. A couple of times when he must have seen a bird he rang general quarters. Everybody rushed to their attack position. He did that twice and became quite a joke among the crew.

Earlier I had referred briefly to Robbie 2, one of the three stewards. Our backgrounds were somewhat different, to any the least. Robbie 2 was born and raised in Harlem, and I in Wilmington, Delaware. A small city that enjoyed a certain ambiance due to the fact that the DuPont Company thrived there since 1802. Their presence brought a disproportionate amount of chemists and engineers and other educated ones to our little city, and for years this helped to have us referred to as to having the highest per capita income in the country. Of course credit goes to the founders of our fair city who arrived nearly 200 years before the DuPont's left France and got things moving along early on. Back to the subject, Robbie 2 and I had a noticeable rapore right off the bat, and we were very open with each other, which I enjoyed very much. For example we were both in the head combing our hair, when Robbie 2 made an interesting observation, and in a very open way, I thought. Robbie 2 said "you stand in front of the mirror encouraging your wave curl to curl more, and I look in the mirror and try to straighten my kinky hair out. Also you go out and sit in the sun to get more tan, and I set in the shade so that I won't get any darker. From then on we were very at ease with each other, and the dialogue flowed comfortably. Another time I walked out on deck and Robbie 2 looked so unhappy I asked him what was bothering him, he said, Damn it, here I set on this ship in the middle of no where, my last ship was based in Scotland and us black guys told the Scottish girls we were American Indians, we had a great time. How's that for sharing? The second Stewart was also a likeable person, but number three was a surly "leave me alone" type. More about him later on, which I was, and just about everybody else was glad to do. He let it be known in a threatening sort of way that he had been a professional boxer. Boxer or not, I had no further interest in him.

The quartermaster told us we should be in Pearl Harbor in 2 or 3 days. Time to get my dress whites washed. There is a washing machine in the head, and Joe Giddio washes all the clothes. When they are finished Joe puts them just outside the door on the three foot round gear box. A four inch thick shaft comes down from above and, through the box and down into the engine room, the shaft controls the anchor winch. After washing, the clothes are laid out around the perimeter of the shaft, the only trouble is, there is grease there. Wouldn't you know, my non regulation bell bottom fine quality material uniform has grease on it? Down to the engine room for a shot of their magic steam, and Voila, A-1 shape.

Our entrance at Pearl Harbor wasn't dramatic like the entrance to Bermuda was. From the states to here had been smooth and pleasant all the way. So here we are, in the submarine base at Pearl. To our left up on a hill is Hickem Field, the airbase. On the other side of the anchorage is battleship row, or at least it was battleship row. There is still smoke coming up, it's a sickening sight, all those powerful ships either sunk or badly wounded. There were a lot of human casualties; some who went down with their ship are still with her....on the bottom. As we say in the sailor's song BLESS THEM ALL. The airfield is still full of holes that haven't been fully repaired. Most of the planes were on the tarmac when the Japs attacked and were destroyed.

I forgot to mention, Joe Giddio was "born in the shadow of the Brooklyn Bridge." He called it something like blood field, some rough area I am told. His father was a good friend of Jimmie Durante, the snooze. Thought that little tidbit might be of interest, "everybody loves Jimmie".

After two days in port Bill Brodie and I made a liberty in Waikiki, first we walked the town, then to the beach. The Royal Hawaiian Hotel had the beach to itself; she was impressive, dressed in bright pink paint, they allowed us to change there into our bathing suits. Bill, having been a native Miamian, wanted to rent surf boards and surf, this was new to me, as a matter of fact, I don't think I had ever heard of it. We rented the boards from a Jap which felt a little uncomfortable, because you have to wonder where his loyalty lies. So we attack the surf with our boards, Bill paddled right out without stopping. The second time he surfed in, I hadn't gotten beyond the breaking waves yet, I was embarrassed to beat the band. Every time I approached the breakers I had to stop for a breath and I would be partially washed in, I never did make it beyond the breakers. Makes me wish that more time had been spent working out with Bill.

Diamond Head is very visible, it makes for a beautiful sight, jutting out of the green Pacific Ocean. Leave it to me to find fault with this "paradise", but I couldn't believe what I saw floating in quantity, Tomato hulks! Campbell soups have a plant somewhere in the area near Diamond Head and this is a daily occurrence. To top it all off, when I continuously kept falling off the board the coral on the bottom cut my foot, and it became very infected. Well, anyway, the weather was beautiful and the sight seeing in a wholly different environment was lots of fun, Nobody had challenged Bill today and we took the train back to the base and sure enough the drunken sailors came rolling out the doors, rolling down the steps to the platform still punching away at each other, it looks like they had a good day in town. I thought that booze was to make you happy; apparently, these guys are happy when they are angry as hell, to each his own. A couple of the men who had been aboard during the attack said, it was a strange day in many ways. For example, in addition to their normal port and starboard liberties there were also others ashore. Most of the gun crews had been allowed ashore, and there weren't an awful lot of others, other than cooks. Does that mean there were few gunners intentionally; or was it just coincidence? Perhaps that question will come up at some later date.

The next time I got to go ashore alone, so I just went to a movie. If there had been some practical way to extend my looking around town it would be welcome, but apparently, public transportation is not available, so I just "people" watched for a while and returned to the ship. There was a poker game going on as usual, so I sat in on the game and had fun watching the bluffers and the raisers trying to beat each other. Joe and Chuck went head to head until you thought they were going to fight, but they were the best of friends and they were just dinging each other for the fun of it. Nobody has seen the gunners mate for 24 hours, maybe he chose to bring on this "strain" and use the clap ruse to get off the ship, or was it just a ruse? We will never know for sure, but I think he has flown the coop because he did not show up last night in our petty officers quarters to sleep. He had been in the service for many years. His favorite expressions were "wherever I hang me hat is me home." The scuttlebutt says we should be moving along in a couple of days. The first thing the crew did when we arrived last week was to off load the aviation fuel and refill with bunker oil, which will permit us to do what the ship was built for. Supply fuel to all of our ships in need, whether in port or at sea. This will be the longest leg of the journey, crossing the balance of the Pacific. I wonder whether it will be one long run, or will there be stopovers, God knows where?

We threw our lines off today and headed back to sea after a last look at the pathetic wrecks the Japs created in battleship row. They are getting theirs according to the news we have been getting. Our shipbuilders are knocking ships out like automobiles.

The ocean remains calm, but we did see a disturbing sight today. In the open sea is a good time for target practice. We came upon a target that had not been sunk. The targets are wooden pieces about three feet square, with an automotive tube for flotation, with a little flag to make it more visible. Now we are several days out of Pearl Harbor, and the nearest island is Johnson Island, but that is behind us. It is an incredible sight, but there are two birds, gulls, on the target, and hundreds, literally hundred of sharks swimming around the target in a semi clock tight circle. The ones inside the circle occasionally jump out of the water and make a grab for the birds. As they finally passed out of sight in the distance, the birds were still alive on their resting spot. It kind of gives you the creeps to see how many could collect in the same spot. You couldn't help but wonder if the ship went down and you didn't get in a lifeboat would the sharks get you?

Fun for everybody. Today we cross the International Date Line. Anybody that has not crossed before gets the treatment. First you get a haircut, which consists of a shear going from front to back down the middle; the reverse of the Indian Mohawk. Of course, it's hilarious when the other ones get it, but it is all done in good fun. Then your head is treated to a message...with axel grease, and if that is not enough, you are blindfold and threatened by King Poseidon for entering his territory and you get whacked with the deck mop. After the ceremony Frank Galante, the ships barber, cut all our hair and shaved our heads completely. We got a kick out of all the shiny baldheads. Poor Robbie 1, he had a head that came up into a pinhead. He was very embarrassed and the crew razzed him all the more about it. To make it worse, the majority of us had fun raising beards, some chose full face beards, which look good on some, and no so hot on others. Then there were a couple of goatees, and different types of mustaches, some kept trimmed and others were wild looking. That was my choice (a mustache). Poor Robbie 1, was so young, and blond, he came up with an ugly scraggly looking thing, a little patch here and there. One morning at breakfast one of the guys told him to get rid of that thing, you're making us all sick, Robbie 1 refused. Tex was called upon in his sleep to supply a few of the crabs he was raising because he hadn't ever bathed willingly. Anyway, whoever the kind soul was that transferred some of Tex's crabs to Robbie's beard were never known. That went too damn far, the kid had to shave his beard, but the way it was done just wasn't right. To close out the beard episode, the prize one was a beauty. It was a full beard, the proud owner was constantly combing it, and it was an extremely healthy BLUE beard.

When I came off the midnight to 4 watch I was tired and a little out of sorts. Our food supply was running low, and it would mean facing those literally stinking dehydrated eggs again. When I arrived at my bunk, lo and behold my least favored crew member was in my bunk, and to top it off, he was crying. It didn't make a damn bit of sense, but by now it wasn't sense I was looking for. So I reached up and grabbed him, after falling the four feet to the deck he bounced a couple of times and as he started to come to his feet I stepped back and prepared for the fight I was expecting. Instead of coming at me he left the room crying like a baby. In the meantime the lights had come on, what the hell is the matter with him, I asked? You have been on this cruise with him for six months, don't you know? No, I don't. He is on dope and his supply has run out and he's suffering withdraw. This was news to me, never heard of it before. So that's why he kept to himself and seemed so contrary. Apparently a couple of the older ones knew about it but kept it quiet. The quartermaster told us he approached the Captain first thing in the morning and told him "I just can't stand being around all these young men, they drive me crazy". By mid morning a battleship was passing us on the starboard side and the Captain had our signalman signal we had a sick man aboard and would like to transfer him. When given the okay we put him in a breeches buoy, shot the line to the wagon and transferred him over. Good riddance, the clever devil. Thank goodness there apparently was no more dope on our ship for him, but there would be an equipped hospital on the big ship. Lord knows what they will do with him, but you have to give the Captain credit this time, he disposed of him fast.

The next occurrence just should not happen. The Ensign who is in charge of the radio people and the signalman (ten years experience), came in and gave me a message to be sent to WAX, our trans Pacific world's most powerful radio station in California. Knowing we could not possibly have that much range, I told him that it could be sent to Guam, and they would pass it on for us. In a nasty way, he said SEND IT like I told you to. There was not a bit of sense in breaking radio silence and risking our ship by telling any lurking enemy where we are, so instead I stood up, pretended to tune the transmitter through its six cycles, and tapped furiously on the key. Finally, I said, "I can't raise them"; he said disgustedly "all right, do it your way then" and stamped out angrily. Then I stood up, shoved the big knife switch that was over my head in, then the antenna was ready to go. After fully tuning the transmitter, I proceeded to send the message to our land station in Guam on their much more powerful radio, and they in turn relayed the massage back to the states.

Our code was a big hush hush top secret. Goldie had told me before that an enlisted man was not to have access to the code machine, which was locked in a closet. This was a TOP secret, but because he couldn't do it on his own, this officer told Goldie enough to start him off, and Goldie studied the book, and from then on had a hand in all the encoding and decodes of our messages......This sort of thing must come about frequently. These persons are referred to as ninety day wonders. There is no way this one or any one else is going to learn in ninety days to be a deck officer, communications, which in addition to us radio girls we have a signalmen with many years experience with signaling with flags or with the blinking light, using Morse code. Well in all fairness, if someone had worked for quite a while, he might be able to pick up the knowledge to be a deck officer if he had considerable leadership ability. The Ensign (90 days) that was put in charge of the gun crew (over 1st class gunner with years of experience) had brains enough to tell his crew "I don't know diddley about this job, but if you fellows will work with me, we should make a good crew, and they were. I am told the services take these fellows with a couple of years in College, studying business, teaching, or whatever, and after ninety days they expect them to "run the job". There is no way it can be done, they should promote from within instead of giving us half-assed untrained people over us. Not to beat a dead horse to death, but by far one of the seamen probably had more education than all the officers combined did. An older fellow (old in his late twenties) old to us 18 to 21 blokes, holds a DOCTORS DEGREE in math and taught it before enlisting. Another seaman left the bank where he was a vice president to come in and do his bit; these people have nothing to prove. Kenneth Dick was the one with the doctorate, oh yes, and he taught math on the college level, and he was quite happy working on the deck.

We are lumbering along at our standard eight knots, sort of like the rabbit and the tortoise. Another beautiful day at sea, not a ship of any description in sight. You know, even in the broad Pacific there are channels that ships adhere to. Our deck, as usual was lightly awash from the little waves coming on board. Since it is warm as usual, why not be down up against the bridge structure and take a pleasant sunbath. So lie down on the warm deck I did, and the water felt as good washing around and occasionally over my warm body. Before I realized what was happening, a "wild wave" they are called, lifted me, I found myself being floated overboard. By this time, my legs were going over the side and I came very much out of the relaxed stupor, and my survival instincts took over. There was a stanchion close enough that I was able to grab it and pull myself back on. In spite of my stupidity my quick reflex saved the day for me. Visions of watching the ship go without me made me promise myself that I would never do a fool thing like that again.

Since my experience a few days ago everything seems rather peaceful, so this is a good time to take up the "battle of proper dress." It was touched on, but not completed. It goes like this, the crew started cutting their dungarees off to make shorts, left their chambray shirts off and in some cases the hat also, after Pearl Harbor it was pretty warm, and our ship was all by itself as usual, because we were too slow to travel in a ten or possibly twelve knot convoy. When the Captain saw these out of uniform crew on deck, and he could see it spreading, he had the yeoman type up orders and attach them to the bulletin board. It read like this, "The uniform of the day will be white hats, chambray shirts and dungarees". These orders were torn off the board and destroyed. It only took a few days for all the crew to follow suit, then the officers liked the idea of being comfortable under the circumstances.

The Captain had one more move; he called for a dress inspection to be carried out on the lower main deck. That meant that our shoes and trouser legs would be awash in the sea water running across the deck. Look, to hell with it, this is not New York, this is mid ocean, and as usual no one in our presence. So I'll be damned if all the officers didn't follow suit. This was too much for the old man so guess what? In a few days he appeared up on the catwalk with his khaki trousers cut down to make shorts. The poor devil was trying to be agreeable and go along with everybody, but one of the guys looked up and laughed at him. He had a big belly, and his hairy glaring white legs did look kind of funny, because we were young and tanned. It's too bad the one person had to embarrass him further. The Captains cabin interconnected with the bridge and the wardroom where the officers ate their meals. He never came out on deck again, except in an emergency situation. Does it remind you of Captain Queeg? A smaller, ordinary little ship, trying his best and having a rotten time of it. The big spit and polish outfits don't get bogged down like this. They have first of all a higher ranking officer who is in a much stronger position because of the support he receives from this battery of officers, the threat of the brig and/or court marshal. The parallel this little ship has with Mr. Roberts is sometimes startling, but we have our good points. Offhand I can't think of anybody who is derelict in their duty; with the possible exception of Tex. Apparently he's okay as helmsmen, but the Officer of the Day is required to stand close to him, and he has been over powered by Tex's odor, and then the OD would make him take a shower while he steered the ship. What a charming couple, that arrogant little executive officer and poor common, pungent Tex, with the bridge all to themselves. The odd couple, one fussy as an old maid, the other couldn't care less.

Chuck opened the batch and stuck his head in, he was about to relieve me, but he said, put her on the speaker and come here a minute. An Island was taking shape ahead; from a distance they appear purple, and kind of hazy. But now as we come closer a small island with not a palm tree on it appeared so barren. The pre invasion bombardment must have been very heavy. Our signalman said the quartermaster told him the Island was named Mog Mog, a small Island belonging to the Marshall Chain. Chuck relieved me and as I watched from the wing of the bridge as we dropped anchor, it only appeared about three feet above sea level. The motor mechanics were busy lowering our motorized lifeboat, and the poop was anybody not on duty could go ashore. Big Bill and Frank Galante came up on the bridge and we piled in the lifeboat.

When we arrived ashore a Marine told us they and the Army had just invaded recently. Already they had laid out football and baseball fields, and there was also a boxing ring. Frank is sitting on one side of Bill and I was on the other. An army guy in the ring announced their man was the Champ of the Marshals, and was there anybody in the U. S. Navy with the guts to take him on. This tall skinny kid jumped up, and he seemed real eager, so they put the gloves on him. The bell rang, they met in the center of the ring and the army champ punched the hell out of the poor kid. They had to stop it before he was hurt badly. The MC said isn't there anybody that can stay a round with our champ? Frank on his side is elbowing Bill in the ribs, and I'm on the other side, urging our man to go in. Bill didn't respond quickly, but he finally got to his feet. He was so big, he looked almost clumsy, but we knew he had played football at the University of Miami before coming in, so he wasn't at all awkward. Good natured Bill finally gave in when we said, "We can't take that crap," Bill, being the good natured giant that he was got to his feet. The referee put the gloves on Bill, the bell rang and the Champ came dancing gracefully across the ring Bill got up slowly, just before the other fighter reached his corner, our boy brought a sizzling right upper cut into the champs jaw. Now I want you to know, lying is not my forte, as God is my witness that former champion followed Bills fist up into the air. His feet were literally three feet off the deck, and that's not all, the poor devil flew clear across the ring and his feet never touched the deck!!!! When he hit the ropes still in the air, he collapsed in a heap as though he didn't have a bone in his body. The referee was awe struck as was everyday else. We had just witnessed what no heavyweight champion had ever done in the history of boxing. One mighty punch and the man flew twenty feet through the air. Bill walked calmly over to the referee to have his gloves removed as nonchalant as ever. This had probably happened before when he fought in the carnival. Frank and I hadn't done a thing except pester him until he went in, but man were we two proud sailor boys. Our Bill was not only champ of the Marshals, but he set a standard nobody NOBODY will ever equal. What an athlete that man is.

It seems to me our next anchorage was in Ulithe, in the Caroline Islands, but I have no recollection of it, didn't amount to much I guess. But I do remember that Yap was close by, and we were told not to drop anything on the deck that would make noise, because we were just over the horizon from Yap, which was held by the Japs. Any metallic noise could be picked up by sonar. After Ulithe, we continued westward, on our way again. A few days later I was on watch when a message came through to bypass the Philippines and set sail for Okinawa.

While on the subject of personalities, I would be remiss if our second cook wasn't mentioned. He is a Kentuckian, just about as pleasant a little man you'll ever come across. Never grouchy like some of us who got bored with it all. Now in all fairness you must realize this little man is trying by himself occasionally to feed seventy seven people under all sorts of conditions. For example, he has an assistant who helps him, and the one day he made the same mistake Anthony made when he threw dirty water into the wind and wetted the Exec. The cook's helper threw a dishpan full of hot cooking oil out the galley porthole, the wind was a bit cranky and it came back in his face and upper body. The poor guy went into shock and we all give our 3rd class corpsman a lot of credit for looking into his treatment and probably saving his life, because he was severely burned. Again, with the use of breeches buoy outfit we were able to transfer him over to a large ship with a hospital. Now when cookie is operating the galley, he has no help. Of course that also applies to the 1st cook. Occasionally when I would come off the 12 to 4 watch my fat little friend would be slaving away in the galley over that miserable hot oil stove. Cookie would take the pans out of the oven, twelve loaves to a pan. He would give the hot bread pan a mighty heave, and the beautiful browned loaves would come cascading out, causing the cock roaches to scatter all over the deck. His arms were broken out from the heat, and you would see the sweat running down his arms into the new batch he was kneading for another twelve loaves. So the next morning at breakfast some clown breaks one of these beautifully browned loaves over his knee, reaches deep inside and pulls a handful of uncooked dough out and throws it up and sticks it on the overhead. Poor good natured cookie stumbled out of the mess hall with tears in his eyes. That damned stove was to blame, that was a little too much even for our buddy the cook.

Sven told us we are only about one thousand miles out of Okinawa at this point. This afternoon a large battle fleet whizzed by us at about 35 knots, wagons, aircraft carriers, cruisers, destroyers, etc., that was quite an impressive show. At the speed they are going they should be in Okinawa tomorrow.

Three days ago, the battle fleet whizzed by us.....what a terrible shock. The aircraft carrier Franklin came limping by terribly shot up. Our signalmen worked with their man on the blinker light as they passed. Their man said hundreds of KAMIKAZE ATTACKED THE SHIPS IN THE HARBOR. The Franklin took many hits; she is barely afloat going to Pear Harbor. That is all he had time for, they continued slowly on their way. Franklin is one of the newest CV flat tops, the beautiful large ones. Small ones have been built that do not hold a candle to these babies. Their signalman said some of the men were blown overboard from all the explosions on deck, and hundreds of kamikaze were shot down. It must have been a terrible battle. We should be there in a couple of days; there is no telling what awaits us.

We pulled into the harbor at Okinawa and were assigned an anchorage position way up inside the harbor near land, only about 300 yards away. Anchored on one side of us is an LST, and on the other the old WW1 Battleship the USS Pennsylvania. Buckner Bay as this huge crescent shaped harbor was renamed, when the marine general was killed in the early days of the invasion. The newer and larger ships are anchored way out at the entrance to the harbor, in case the Japs would attack, and they would not be bottled up in the harbor. You can see a lot of the damage from the kamikaze just the other day. Scuttlebutt claims there are around 2000 planes on the bottom here, some that were shot down, and some that hit our ships.

Our ship, being so close to the shore, like so many others, must maintain a fore and aft, and another port and starboard watch each equipped with an automatic rifle, The Japs are building rafts out of bamboo, loading a bomb on board and paddling out and ramming anyone that does net shoot them first, at the water line and of course sinking them. I understand it has not been very effective, but who wants to be caught unprepared?

We have only been here a few days and already a typhoon came through last night. All the major ships in the outer harbor are riding it out at sea. The smallest ships to face it outside were the destroyers. Even at that, they have been known to sink in a typhoon. All the rest of us take our chances in the inner harbor. The waves coming in from the sea and pushing up on the shallow harbor became huge, like 60 feet high. Our little tanker fared better than a lot of others, I think because four fifths of our decks only rise about a foot or so above the water, and do not create much windage. The balance, which is the house or living quarters, is all we have projecting up into the wind. As a huge six story building size would roll in from the sea we would ride up one side like climbing on a roller coaster, reach the top, and head ass over head down the other side of the wave. Our ship had two anchors splayed out on about a 30-degree angle, and our engine going two thirds ahead just to hold on, but fortunately, we did hold on, but several others did not. You could see remains along the shoreline, sunk and destroyed. You see the banks along the shore are covered with coral, so when ships and their crews were thrown forcefully upon the coral there were no survivors. We were damned lucky and maybe its time to give old..... CRASH BOAT COLLINS SOME CREDIT, for a change. The second and third day's bodies kept popping up, all crab eaten. Of course, you feel terrible for the dead, and for our boys working the deck had to pull out the ones that came our way.

Today they selected me to go ashore and pickup the mail at NAHA, on the other side of the Island, where fighting I think is still going on. So, I was given a 45 to strap on, and a boat was sent from shore to pick me up. There is only one road on the island, which I believe runs around the outer perimeter of the island. So, here goes, to my left is the harbor, and on my right, there is a bank with about a 60 degree angle and about 20 feet wide. Shortly before I even got started, a Jap family approached from the opposite direction. There were two tiny adult civilians and two children. The adults had long sticks over their shoulders with a small bucket at each end, going for water, I assumed. What happened next really shocked me; the hillside had signs in both Japanese and English warning about this hillside. The mines had not been cleared yet, this was a minefield!! As they approached me within about 50 yards they detoured into the minefield and as they passed they bowed toward me, continually facing me until they past, saying repeatedly "ah Joe ah Joe". A jeep picked me up about this time going to NAHA. The fellow looked miserable as the devil, so subtle me I say; you look miserable what is wrong. He told me he is a Seabee, and the Japs fly over every night (I know, because they go over the harbor very high) night after night and they bomb the airfield at NAHA. So everyday they have to spend 16 hours repairing the holes they have made. Then he said sarcastically, in our spare time we took some drums and made a shower, hoping to get clean for a change, but before they were able to use it the typhoon blew it down. I then asked him about the Jap experience I had, he said they thought you were going to kill them. Some Jap soldiers put civvies on, sneak into our sleeping quarters at night, and stab us to death. Therefore, during the day if any Jap civilian gets close, we knock his brains out with our rifle butts, and then he cannot kill us in our sleep. He dropped me off just outside NAHA.

Shortly I came upon what the army refers to as a latrine; the navy term is a head. This was a building just off the edge of the road;

it was about 20 feet square, with some sort of wainscoting about 3 feet high surrounding it. Nature called so I walked in, due to my somewhat different upbringing I was startled, to say the least. After thinking it over for a minute, I pulled the old boy out and relieved myself. The women ignored me and I paid them the same courtesy, actually, I suppose this method is natural for them.

NAHA had of course been their capital city, until our bombardment. To say it was serious would be a big under statement. In the entire small city there was only one building left standing. Just picture a small southern town in the states demolished, except for the U. S. new headquarters. The navy did a through job of pre invasion bombing and shelling. The mail was turned over to me in the headquarters building and I was able to get another jeep back promptly. When finished the driver told me they swipe the rotor, so some jeep will usually be available.

Back at the wharf, I spent a little time looking at the numerous caves about 100 feet from the water. You could get a better view than what was available from the ship. They looked dark and foreboding inside; I did not go in, just peered in from the outside. One of the tenders took me back to the ship, and I had the pleasure of giving out the mail this time. The fellows were very glad to get it. It has been a while; letters from home can be a big morale lift, of course that goes without saying.

Coming off the 4 to 8 watch, I am usually somewhat irritable. There usually is not enough traffic to keep you active and around 5AM about time for the first glimmering of the sun, I am so overcome with sleep I have to hit my head against the bulkhead to stay awake. The prospect of those literally stinking dehydrated eggs again for breakfast is not conductive to good humor. We have not taken on stores for god knows how long. According to Sven on the bridge, we had a turn recently when the supply ship came out from the States. Somebody, maybe on Admiral on a flat top or somebody with a lot more gold than our little two stripper, calls the supply ship over and takes our turn. If it weren't for the "K" rations I had been stealing from the lifeboat hanging conveniently off the wing of the bridge, I would be damned near starved. Had we been hit in mid ocean the ones in that lifeboat might have starved. That's called survival. So anyway, I come off the 4 to 8 watch and went to the galley. Took my tray of the unmentionable to the table and sat down next to one of the boys from the black gang. These guys made good friends to have. When the masterminds on the bridge said we had to shower in sticky old seawater, these boys made others and me a key to turn on the fresh water they made from seawater. They could make a lot more fresh water than was needed, THERE WAS NO SHORTAGE. So as we were getting settled a huge steel arm, about 8 inches in diameter and 20 feet long, came through the side of the ship and ran right down the table, right down the middle, mind you. The table was connected to the bulkhead, and there were six of us on either side of the table. This big arm is swung out from the side of the ship in port to prevent the small supply boats from bumping them. As it turned out we were very lucky, no one was hit. We all jumped up and ran up on the catwalk facing the bridge. One brave soul was shaking his fist at the Captain, old CRASH BOAT and yelled, you crazy son of a bitch, are you trying to kill us? Granted, that was not very good behavior, of course that was not the first time he had put our lives at risk. He never would allow the quartermaster authority; he stood by the controls and barked orders to the helmsman. We careened off more than one other that we were also pumping oil to. He never developed a feel for pulling alongside another vessel, and he would not delegate the authority to someone who could do it. Oh! Boy! Another day another dollar. The outspoken one was not punished for his outburst. The incident was never mentioned again anyway.

Oh great, another typhoon will be on us by tomorrow, the weather man said. Being somewhat experienced should help us this time. The crew is tying up rope lines to help walk in the open spaces on deck, where the wind is the strongest. There were a couple of rather bad falls on those windy wet decks. We certainly don't want any broken bones if it can be avoided. The last General Quarters we had Fred, in the excitement jumped from the flying bridge 12 feet down below, his feet were bruised. Old Fred must have faked that injury as long as he could; he carried it off pretty good for a banker. The ships anchors are splayed out, and dug in good. Nothing is being left lying around on deck that could get loose and maybe kill somebody. I hope all the surrounding ships are taking precautions as well. During the last storm some ships got loose and went up on the shore and broke up. Maybe a lesson has been learned which will prevent that from happening again. I for one don't intend to cross that open deck area unless I have to. It was exciting, though, when the wind lashed water blowing horizontally struck you in the face and it stung from the force of it. Batten down the hatches, here she comes. The day was beautiful until mid afternoon the wind started up, and the storm clouds blew in on us. The ships engine is running at a reduced speed up until now, but as the wind and waves build up, so will the ships engine, so as to help take some of the strain off the anchors, our lives are at stake.

This typhoon pretty well paralleled the first one, high winds, bring high tides with it. It looked to be a soggy mess on shore. Okinawa seems to be dust up to your ankles, or after rain, and especially typhoon rains, it's a slogging mud hole. I don't know how the ships at sea made out, but they are continually returning, and no sinking has come to light as yet. The ones that are most vulnerable are the Destroyers, they're not too brainy and should they be turned broadside to wind and wave, they could flip over, or come off one and dive bow first into the following one. The bigger heavier ones just seem to be able to bully their way through. That vicious coral studded shoreline is littered with debris as far as you can see, but no major ships in sight, so I hope that means no bodies in two or three days. That makes for a very sorry sight, one not easily forgotten.

Oh yes, I forgot to mention, while ashore for the mail a couple of stake bodied trucks came by me on the road back. They were jammed full of what appeared to be giants. They were prisoners, but surprisingly not tiny Japs but these big mean looking buggers. One of the Marines nearby said they were Koreans, a giant mountain variety who would fight for pay. There were only a couple of soldiers guarding them; it made me a little uneasy. If those big bastards were to overpower the two guards and come spilling out toward me I'd damn sure learn what war was about. Theses guys were 6 foot 6 or better and I would guess about 250 pounds. Anyway they passed by and went on their way.

As was mentioned before, the invasion of Okinawa started on the other side of the island. After the extremely heavy naval bombardment the marines came ashore and became in a fierce battle to first take the airfield, and then start across in a terrible hand to hand effort to finish off the Japs.

This didn't take place overnight. The battle had already been going on for weeks, but this one day I'm off watch relaxing on deck and here come the Jap soldiers, heading our way. They had three choices it appeared, they could stand and fight at the waters edge, they could go into the caves, or drown. They chose the caves.

Warnings are out on a third typhoon. That afternoon as the first mild winds started through, all the major ships at the mouth of the harbor took off and went to sea. Some of them came in to the fuel dock and topped off their tanks, only one ship at a time could be serviced. All afternoon a Dutch troop ship kept signaling for a chance to take on fuel. He was consistently refused. Our signalman who was manning the blinker light and was aware of what was going on between the American authorities and the Dutch ship told us late in the afternoon as the storm started to show it self more, the Dutch troop ship gave up. He couldn't go to sea without enough fuel, so he finally bunkered down and dropped his hooks about 500 yards to the north and battened down for the storm to follow. At late afternoon the winds were already gaining strength and getting uglier. All of a sudden two of the gas barges that are kept at the dock area in case a supply ship brings more aviation fuel than they can currently handle, the surplus will be laid off in the barges so that the tanker can move on. So here come two gasoline barges looking as though they are going to ram us. With the wind pushing them at about 15 miles per hour in the harbor they were frightening, more so than the storm itself. Somehow providence allowed them to miss everybody and disappear beyond all the vessels in our area. That was a very hairy situation, until they had gone by. This is developing into a giant of a storm. The quartermaster told us the barometer has already fallen as far as the reading at the peak of the #2 typhoon. It wasn't more than a few minutes later we saw a PC, the

125 foot wooden boat that looks like a private yacht. Remember, I mentioned them when in Miami, and that we had given some to the Russians, and the rest at the time were being loaded aboard ships and taken to the Pacific for limited use in patrolling for subs. Now, back to the problem at hand, the boat is drifting our way, they are about 30 feet away when they shot us a monkey fist. Our boys did a great job of pulling in the line and they managed to get their hawser ever the niggerhead in the stern. The vessel, slipped in behind us as the slack took up and she appeared to be okay. The Captain appeared on the scene. He spent what looked like a thoughtful moment looking at the hook up, then issued an order. Cut that hawser. We the crew were horrified. We put ourselves in their place; I guess and wanted them to hang on. The Captain shouted this time "Cut that f...ing hawser". One of the boys took a fire axe and cut their life line. I ran to the radio shack, I knew their radio operator would be broadcasting on emergency channel 500. Chuck had taken the earphones off and put it on the speaker. They were about to go on the rocks, the man on the radio was yelling "For Christ Sake help, we're going up on the rocks". When they were holed the generator must have quit, a much weaker signal came on, that had to be their battery operated emergency radio. The poor fellow said "My God we're going down", and they were his last words before they all must have been torn apart on that treacherous coral shoreline. Several of us had enough at that time and we went inside and just sat glumly up against a bulkhead and tried not to cry. So, I went out into the storm again so as not to make a fool of myself.

Now it is midnight, and the typhoon is really upon us. The winds went from 80 to 175 miles per hour, with gusts up to 200 MPH. The huge rollers coming in from the open sea are the size of 8 story buildings, so we are back on the roller coaster. A slow climb up, come over the top and skitter down the other side, hoping she doesn't increase the angle a bit and simply dive under the water. This is the storm of storms. As in the previous typhoon, the wind is blowing horizontally, with such force it hurts your face when it bits. This is a night to remember.

The alarm goes out!! The Dutch troop ship that was denied space at the refueling dock has broken loose and is out of control and coming our way. This is a 500 footer bearing down on us. Her huge anchors broke loose, and are jumping across the bottom, each link of the anchor chain is bigger than a mans fist, but it's shaking like a piece of string, real flexible. The ocean liner is only about 150 yards away, it looks like a crash!! Are we moving? I thought I saw the stern more a little to the port. It did! It did! With our two anchors splayed out as before and going two thirds ahead just to hang on; yes I can see it now. Our stern is swinging hard a port. The huge ship is almost upon us now, I think the swing we took is going to give us a <u>few feet</u> of clearance, but now our concern is their port anchor jumping along the bottom, and it's going to cross over the path of our starboard anchor. If their anchor catches our anchor line and drags us, we're goners. Hooray!....We are lucky SOBs. Their anchor must have jumped right over ours, because it passed over the area our anchor line has to be in. Some would say we are blessed; perhaps we enjoyed a bit of each this time. Lots of other dammed good men weren't so fortunate. If I live to be a hundred I will have to share in the guilt of twelve men we might well have saved. On the other hand, Crash Boat Collins came to the fore and saved our ass this time for sure. This has been a night straight out of hell, let's hope this is it. The winds and waves are still with us, so we'll just have to keep our fingers crossed for a few more hours.

Life must go on. As I pass the galley on the way to a 4 to 8 watch there's good natured old cookie throwing the bread pans across the deck. The cockroaches scurrying as the beautiful brown loaves slide across the deck. By the time my watch is finished the news starts coming in. Two destroyers went down, there is no word as yet how many men were fished out. The odds are stacked up for bad news, I am afraid. The shoreline is covered with all sorts of ships and debris, just as far as you can see. The Jap soldiers are being pushed toward us in larger quantity now. The ones that are not killed are holing up in the caves; they were told if they were captured they would be tortured before being shot, so there aren't many of them who surrender. I'm told that hundreds of civilians are jumping off a cliff rather than be captured. At this point I'm not sure whether they mean here or somewhere else. In going for the mail I went around the outer perimeter of the island. There was no cliff in view when I was ashore. Scuttlebutt isn't always correct, anyway.

At breakfast this morning the subject is the storm, of course, said to be the biggest one in modern times. Old Crash Boat Collins stock was up because of his great move to port, which we feel sure, saved a disaster that would have done us in. Which goes to show, nobody can be wrong all the time. The soldiers and marines are back at their job again this morning, firing up into the caves, because the Japs won't come out. About every fifth bullet is a tracer, which lights so that they can better direct their fire. It's a pretty sight at night, that along with napalm, followed by the dense black smoke. This thing can't last much longer. That silly little man on the white horse better quit soon, or the invasion that's to come will involve him personally. That would be a fitting end to this damned mess.

When you scan this huge harbor full of our ships it gives you a feeling of both pride and tremendous power, and it makes me proud to have been an insignificant part of it, one in ten million. The greatest fighting force is the history of the world. Again, in looking around this harbor a strange thought occurs to me. If this immense fleet were lined up 100 yards apart, and touched the Island of Japan with their bows, went full ahead forward they could push the whole damned aggressive people and their island into the sea.

As usual, when off watch and not sleeping I'm out on deck. Approaching the harbor on their return to Naha our fighter planes are completing their patrol. Then I notice the last one peel off and start a wide sweep of the harbor. For Christ Sake! It's a kamikaze. Just one crazy damned Jap; he chooses his victim and starts his power dive. His target, the USS Pennsylvania, which is 200 yards off our starboard side. There's an LST anchored off our port side, and he's the only ship in the harbor to realize what's going on. They have their quad 40's locked on him, you can see his tracers, but the Jap is not being hit. As the kamikaze gets closer the LST fire starts coming our way. The Jap passes about 20 feet over our stern, and hit's the dear old Pennsylvania right on the waterline. She listed about 20 degrees to port, but they were to keep the old battleship that fought in two world wars afloat. The kamikaze hit right at the officers wardroom, they told us later there were 7 officers killed. The Jap had apparently dropped down from a cloud and fell in behind our last fighter plane, which couldn't see him. Once again our luck held up. That Jap must have been very anxious to die for the emperor and taken off on his own. The last time there had been over 500 of them, that's the same group that shot the Franklin up so badly, as well as many others. That was just a couple of days before our arrival at Okinawa, that's one time being so slow paid off. The USS Oconee has indeed was one lucky little ship.

The killing continues to go on ashore Japs are still being pushed in our direction. Of course I don't see all of the fighting sitting out here on the ship, several hundred yards away from some of it. The action pertaining to the caves though is in our direct line of sight. I haven't seen any more of those giant mountain Koreans, though. There was only a small group employed by the Japs for their furious appearance, I expect. There would appear to be a lull, the nightly bombing of the airfield at Naha still continues, but no more kamikaze have shown up. One thing I've been thankful of, we finally got our turn of provisions, fresh fruits and vegetables, meat, butter, etc. We had gotten down to an ice cream scoop of rice, it came to a head the other day when the 1st cook was plopping the rice on our trays, and Bill extended his tray and received his little scoop of rice. He told the cook to put more on his tray, when the cook said move on he sat his tray down, hit the cook a mighty blow, and put a couple more scoops on his tray. The cook woke up in a couple of minutes and he was crying, he ran topside to talk to the officers and tell what happened. Nobody dared come down, and the whole thing just sort of blew over. Would you dare to chastise an angry gorilla? I sure wouldn't. This was entirely out of character for Bill, for a full year he hadn't shown anger. But I think this meant more than just another missed meal, he knew better than most how this skimpy diet was beginning to take its toll, and he lost his cool this one time. That's all behind us now; we're being fed much better now, thank goodness. It took 20 pounds off me; the last time I was at this weight was at age fourteen. It was during the depression and after one of my Mothers well cooked meals my Father was outraged, because I had eaten a whole box of cereal after a good dinner. As I look back now, he must have thought I was an awful glutton! In hindsight; I'd have to agree with him. Puberty, what a strange time of life. A whole box of cereal, that is. Eating boxes wasn't quite my style.

Life aboard ship goes on. The card games in the galley still going on, give these guys a "Cup A Joe" and a few bucks and the cards come out. Some of our drinking members got hold of "torpedo juice" they called it. We do not have any torpedoes of course, but there must be some raw alcohol they use in the engine room. They seasoned it with Vitalis hair lotion, to make it palatable??? They were going up and down the passageways in the middle of the night, a hoopin and a hollering. That pure alcohol must give you a hell of a hangover, because they sure are morose today. You're taking your life in your hand if you dare address them in a loud voice. No work from the wardroom gang, so I guess that will be overlooked.

Bill still works out regularly, five times a week, with the Friday one being a very heavy workout. Goldie occasionally blows his sax on the fantail, sometimes joined by Art Sporu on the bongo drums. That's good stuff, almost as good as the time I took a date to Pottstown, PA. This was the first time, at 16, that I was going to a dance with the big time orchestra. When I stepped up to the entrance door and flung it open and Benny Goodman's band blasted at us and I was in pig heaven. That was a tremendous thrill for my date and me. Jitterbugging? Oh! Man, we were cool cats that night. Benny drove us bunch of kid's nuts with the great orchestra and his inspired clarinet playing.

Now back to the present. No more Japs arriving on the scene, but our men are still giving them occasional shots of gunfire and napalm, to try to bring them out dead or alive I guess. The tracer bullets still glow at night. The Jap bombers are not flying overhead every night on their way to bomb the airfield at Naha. Everybody is saying something's going on I sure hope so. If we have to invade Japan there will be an awful lot killed. The feeling among the men a million allied lives and a lot more Japs, both soldiers and civilians.

I am kind of enjoying the little lull that we are in right now. The radio is not as demanding as it had been, and things are even quieter on shore. You do not see much of the Japs these days. We copy the Fox Schedules that contain all the orders from Washington. They are communicated to California to WAX, which I think was mentioned before as the most powerful radio station in the world. The orders, etc., come in groups of five apparently garbled, such as mzdxu. These are the unbroken codes that none of the Axis Nations could ever break. In case of a hit my job was to obtain the locked up code book, which had lead secured to the back of it and if sinking were threatened, I was to heave it overboard. Chuck was to seize the portable radio and take it with him to the lifeboat. Prior to that, I was assigned as the bridge talker. My job there was to stand next to the Captain, he would give me the orders for the engine room and the 40 millimeter forties antiaircraft and the 3 inch 50s. We had one of those forward and one aft, Big Bill was first loader on one of them. He made quite a reputation among his gun crew; they were a pretty good size shell. Instead of a grab, lift and shove in the breech as an ordinary man would do, Bill would grab it as it was passed to him there was only one continuous motion. Grab and shove, which of course would mean more rapid fire in a fight.

Something else I had overlooked earlier. Kenny Dick who I mentioned earlier as being the best-educated man on the ship holds a Doctor of Math degree and is only a lowly seaman. Ken was called up to the bridge, they had taken a message, which would allow one man from the ship to go to Officers Candidate School. When it was offered to him, he told us he politely refused. When they became insistent and he still refused they asked him why he was not pleased he said "because I don't want to be a prick like you guys". End of conversation. Kenny had no aspirations for the peacetime Military. He probably figured he could do a lot better with his education; anyway, he seemed to enjoy his seamen's job, working on deck.

Word is going around that a new extremely powerful bomb was dropped on Japan yesterday. There's a lot of excitement aboard ship. Of course heavy conventional bombing didn't seem to discourage them, hopefully this will make a difference. The alternative, invade the Japanese homeland of these fanatic nuts is a most unwelcome thought, there has to be a better way. Hundreds of thousands of my generation have been killed and maimed already.

We are told a second Atomic bomb has been dropped on Japan, and there is talk of a possible surrender. At least there is supposed to be a lot of discussion about it, so let us hope so. It would be wonderful to stop the killing and be able to go home. From this distance home seems about as near as the moon.

SURRENDER!!!! HOT DAMN!!! The Japs are about to sign an unconditional SURRENDER. What a happy day this is for our little ship. You can count on it; our drinking contingent will raise hell tonight. We all will, in our different ways want to celebrate this happy day.

A few days following the Official Papers signing, we were told how to tote up our points toward discharge. Length of service, amount of sea duty is the main requisites, and married men gain points. Lucky me!!! Just about enough points to be discharged when I get home. As soon as transportation is available on a troop ship away I go. I could not be happier.

Three weeks have gone by, and my time has finally come. My sea bag is packed, and all the good byes have been said, a ride ashore is on the way. A final wave to my friends, most of these fellows will have to stay aboard and bring the ship back to either Pearl Harbor or the west coast of the good old U.S.A. I wish they were coming along with me, these men will be missed, they are a great bunch.

A tent has been assigned to several others and me. The APA, that is to take us across the Pacific is in port and will load up tomorrow. She is about 500 feet, and to tell you the truth, this looks like one beautiful vessel. The Hospital ship HOPE is also in port, picking up the wounded and taking them home. Some shattered, and some with limbs missing. God bless them for what they have given, I feel so damned lucky.

This baby seems so huge compared to the Oconee. There are about 3,000 of us being returned, plus the crew. All the services are represented, but nobody gives a damn what branch the others are from, we are all going home. The bunks are four high again, I chose #3. If you remember, I volunteered four times to "get a ship going somewhere", damned if I did not do it again. They wanted a few to lug the beef etc., up from the freezer to the galley a couple of decks above. Turns out it was a cinch, and this gave you the privilege of eating first, after the crew. That worked out fine, because there were three sittings, and the food was not bad. I was hungry as could be.

There were crap games all over the main deck. Having played a bit of crap back home for dimes and quarters, these games were for dollar bills and more, so I was content to watch. My little nest egg was going to remain intact until I got home. The ship itself was a pleasure, we are moving along between 16 to 18 knots, twice the speed of the Oconee. There are plenty of people to talk to; it seemed always to be "where are you from" not where you have been. They have all seen plenty, and did not care to discuss it. Everybody was in a happy mood, and with good reason.

The sea was "Pacific" all the way up to now. We are traveling the "great Northern route", which means you are in the Baring Sea, between Russia and Alaska. It is cold, feels good for a change, somewhat refreshing. The water is a little rough in these Northern climes. A lot of these fellows fought with guns and sabers, but they don't have their sea legs, and they're also getting sick. We eat standing up at these long tables, if you don't hang on to your tray it will move as the ship rolls. So this fellow allows his tray to move as the ship rolls, and as luck would have it his tray stops two neighbors away. This poor guy pukes at the sight of it right in the tray, which is returned to the sender on the next roll. The poor guy may have been holding up reasonably well up until now, but he has to succumb and makes a dash for the deck and the rail. Unfortunately there are two fellows hanging over the rail below his, and he sprays them unintentionally, they are mad as hell, of course, but too sick to move, so that's how it ends. I hope they weren't formally friends.

As we approach what I think is near the apex of this Northern route we come across three or four mines that have broken loose from a harbor north of us, and they're heading out to the open sea, Their gunner gets target practice, the ship stops while he shoots them. It makes quite an explosion. This brings to mind the mine field as we entered Bermuda harbor under tow that was a hairy one, indeed.

Back into the calm Pacific waters and we soon approached the California coast. Boy did it look good! We were berthed in the Kaiser Shipyard. They had completely stopped production of new liberty ships a couple of months ago. They served us a couple of meals, very good meals, and we were on our way the next day aboard buses, heading North was all we could ascertain. After a long bus trip we arrived at a Marine Base, Camp Pendleton, in the state of Washington. They put us in Quonset huts for the night. The first person to get up said "my god, there's a mountain in our back yard". We had arrived at midnight and hadn't seen Mt. Rainer; it shone in the morning sunlight and was overpoweringly beautiful. We were told it was about 150 miles away, what a magnificent site to see.

Things are moving fast now, first thing this morning we were put aboard a train heading EAST. Got to give Uncle Sam a 10 for planning this return trip. The connections have been swift and smooth. The final leg of our journey halfway around the world is coming to a close. The previous leg, from Okinawa to California took sixteen days. Our ship must have taken a couple of months including stops in the Marshals and the Carolines.

For a kid that had never been further from home than Philadelphia to the north, and Washington D. C. to the south, this has been quite an experience. I was privileged, to share a lot with my shipmates, who were a great bunch of people. They will always be a treasured memory.

The train trip through the Rocky Mountains is very beautiful. As we move along you get views of snow capped mountains on one side, then from the other you see breathtaking views down into the valleys and rivers, along the floor thousands of feet down. Not to mention the millions of snow covered trees mile after mile. The train trip is the icing to the cake. On the way home.

The next stop is Philadelphia, where it all started. Upon arrival, discharge from the Military and then........Home at last.

New York to Okinawa Slooooooooly

New York to Okinawa Slooooowly